THE NEAT
GUI[
BRIGHTON'S HISTORY

Christopher
Horlock

S.B. Publications

By the same author

Brighton, the Century in Photographs Volume 1
Brighton, the Century in Photographs, Volume 2
Brighton and Hove Then and Now, Volume 1
Brighton and Hove Then and Now, Volume 2
Brighton: The Sixties

First published in 2003 by
S B Publications
Telephone: 01323 893498
fax: 01323 893860
email: sales@sbpublica-
tions.swinternet.co.uk
Reprinted in 2005
Reprinted in 2010

© 2003 Christopher
Horlock
The moral right of the
author has been asserted

ISBN 185770 26 1 1

Typeset by JEM Editorial,
JEMedit@AOL.com

Printed by Pageturn Ltd,
East Sussex, BN3 7EG.
Tel: 01273 821500

INTRODUCTION

This guidebook is for people in a hurry. It's a quick, easily digested history of the City of Brighton, with most of the interesting bits included and a lot of the boring bits left out. It's written too, assuming the reader doesn't know an awful lot about history, so everything's explained and clearly spelt out. But it's restricted to what's known as the Old Town area of Brighton, the famous Royal Pavilion estate, plus a place called Old Steine. These three sites are the city's historic heart and soul and where most of the really intriguing things have happened over the years. They're all connected and are within a few minutes' walking distance of one another, so there's no hassle finding them.

THE MAP

The Old Town area is a rectangle of streets bounded by the seafront (King's Road), North Street, East Street and West Street. Within this rectangle are other old streets like Middle Street, Black Lion Street, Ship Street and Duke Street, plus a network of ancient walkways, known as The Lanes. All have stories to tell. Old Steine (usually just The Steine) and the Pavilion estate are just to the north-east of all this.

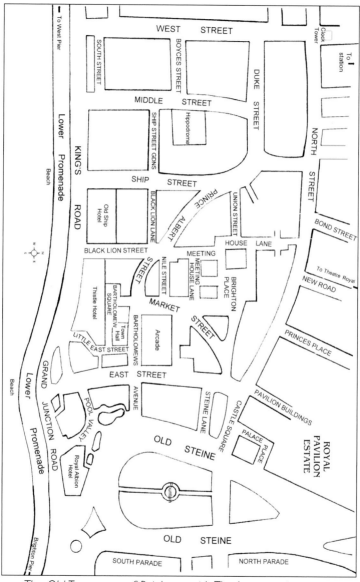

The Old Town area of Brighton, with The Lanes at its centre

ANCIENT TIMES

When Brighton first came into existence no one really knows. There are ancient hill camps on the outskirts of the city (the one at a place called Hollingbury, well north of Brighton, is the best to visit, if you're interested), Bronze age relics have been discovered and the Romans left behind a small villa, but the first real settlement, on the site of Brighton today, seems to have been made in Saxon times (say, 480 AD). East Street, West Street and North Street probably emerged in the thirteenth or fourteenth centuries and the street pattern in between, that makes up the Old Town area, dates from a substantial rebuilding of the town in the mid-1500s, after being burnt to the ground by the French.

Brighton has had more than forty different names that we know about. In the Domesday survey of 1086, ordered by William I, after winning the Battle of Hastings, the place was called Bristelmestune. Then, the town's value was rated the equivalent of 400 herring fish and the population is thought to have numbered about 500 people in all. Later it became Brithampton. Brighthelmstone was the name for most of the eighteenth century, but plain, simple Brighton was being used from the late 1700s, and this name was officially taken in 1810. All of these names seem to derive from *Beorthelm's Tun*; Beorthelm being a Saxon ruler, the 'tun' being his farm or land. To avoid a lot of confusion, this guide uses the name Brighton whatever period is being discussed.

TUDOR TIMES

The earliest picture of Brighton we have is a drawing of 1545, shown opposite, when Henry VIII ruled England. Then, the place was called Brithampton.

In it a fleet of ships from France is attacking and burning the town. This was a terrorist raid, made to 'persuade' the English, who still had possession of Calais, to get out of France. They'd held onto this, despite the Hundred Years' War and Joan of Arc clearing the English from the rest of France a century before. The town was, seemingly, burnt to the ground.

East Street (right), West Street (left) and North Street (top) are all

shown, as is the church of St Nicholas, on a hill above the town; this survived the attack and still stands today. Fishermen's cottages can be seen down on the beach, fishing dominating the town's economy at this time. At least one of the attacking ships sank and its remains lie in the sea just west of Brighton's Marina. A plate giving details is fixed to railings on the promenade. Several items from the wreck have been recovered, including cannons and an anchor.

Following this assault (and previous raids), the town was forti-fied in 1559, during the early reign of Elizabeth I (when Calais was

The Blockhouse seen in the centre of the town's defensive wall

back in French possession). Then, it's recorded, the town was said to possess eighty fishing vessels, 400 mariners and 10,000 nets and lines.

A huge defensive wall was built along the part of the town facing the sea, with a castle (called the Blockhouse) in the centre. This had ten cannons, which could be fired as any enemy approached. Several gates led to the beach area, but hardly any fishermen lived down there then and it's pretty obvious why!

Brighton wasn't attacked again, in a huge way anyway, so these defences were never tested, but were still in place when the Spanish Armada of 1588 sailed eastwards along the south coast, pursued by the full might of the English navy. Spain was attempting a full-scale invasion of England at this time, ordered by its king, Philip, who wanted to restore the Catholic faith throughout the country, and who was fed up with sea-dogs like Francis Drake

Collapse of the Blockhouse

attacking Spanish ships and making off with their cargoes of treasure. It's tempting to wonder if the cannons of the Blockhouse were fired at the fleeing Spanish, if they wandered close to Brighton's shoreline, but there's no record of this, and the fleet was eventually wrecked around the northern coasts of the country.

FALL AND RISE

Brighton remained a small but very significant fishing town during all these early dramas and continued that way until the mid-1700s. Fishing took place locally, of course, but the fleet mainly headed for the east coast of England, fishing in the North Sea off Scarborough and Yarmouth.

From the mid-1600s, there was massive erosion along the south coast of England and much of Brighton fell into the sea. A huge storm swept away the entire 'lower town' (the beach community) in 1703 and there was another storm two years later which wrecked much of the 'upper town' (the community on the cliff). The population subsequently fell by a third, there was economic collapse and the place resembled a ghost town. Further erosion made what was left of the old defensive wall crack up and the Blockhouse eventually split in half and tumbled onto the beach.

Daniel Defoe, the author of *Robinson Crusoe,* made a tour of England in the early 1700s and came to Brighton about 1720. Passing through, he considered the town to be in such a state of utter dilapidation, it wasn't worth spending any money rebuilding it. Another eyewitness, a man named Dunvan, said the town looked like 'a place bombarded by the enemy'.

Well Brighton was truly down, but it wasn't out, and its extraordinary salvation was a case of 'come the hour, come the man …'

THE SEA-WATER CURE

It was in 1750 that a physician from the county town of Lewes, Dr Richard Russell, published a paper extolling the virtues of seawater bathing as a cure for all manner of 'human ills', including glandular problems, tumours and 'eruptions'. He claimed that drinking seawater whitened the teeth (due to the salt), kept the head clear and the bowels regular ('a pint a day,' he enthused, 'will give three or four sharp stools'). He even

Dr Richard Russell

recommended relaxation techniques before undertaking seawater bathing, an idea years ahead of its time, but also, unfortunately, like an alchemist of old, he came up with some revolting pills for various ailments, made from crab's eyes, bits of coral, viper's flesh, snails, tar and wood lice.

Russell wasn't the first to suggest that sea bathing was a healthy undertaking; in fact, Brighton was already something of a spa town by now, following major rebuilding after all those storms. But little of importance was going on and few amenities were available for visitors. Russell's ideas became hugely influential almost overnight, leading to a substantial influx of wealthy invalids arriving in Brighton (by stage coach), to try the sea-water cure. Many really did seem to benefit from a 'dip in the briny', probably from absorbing the iodine in it and because it acted as a mild disinfectant (remember, people didn't wash much then and were a pretty filthy lot).

Straight away, the townsfolk of Brighton saw they could make money from these visitors and soon the fishing fleet was jostling for space on the beach with bathing machines. These were huts on wheels, pulled by horses to the water's edge, from which those about to bathe in the sea could privately change into suitable

A dip in the briny cured 'all manner of ills'

Richard Russell's house at the water's edge and the Royal Albion Hotel plaque

'flannels' (baggy bathing suits) and then step out straight into the water, down a small flight of steps. All for a small fee of course. The good fisher-folk had their eye to the main chance again, when they realised these people might need 'assistance' when bathing; so 'dippers and bathers' were established, people who would aid the whole process of getting in and out of the sea, to give safe – and full – immersion, ensuring the right kind of benefits. They also gave swimming lessons (few people from towns or cities could swim then, it seems), no doubt sold these visitors their choicest cuts of fish and started pleasure trips in their boats (let's hope they cleaned them up a bit first!). Most audacious of all was the bottling of seawater and selling it in London, as 'oceanic fluid'. An advertisement in a London magazine of 1756 announced that seawater, from Brighthelmstone, in Sussex, could be bought at the Talbot Inn in Southwark. Later it was for sale at many other places.

Russell moved to Brighton, 'just down the road' from Lewes, and built a mansion near the water's edge, where he could minister to his patients personally. At the rear was a large beach area where his exclusive bathing machines operated. After his death in 1759 (he didn't enjoy fame for long), his house was used for a number of different purposes until demolition in 1823. The Royal Albion Hotel subsequently occupied the site; it still stands at the southern end of Old Steine, opposite Brighton Pier, much enlarged and extended now. There is a plaque on the side facing the sea, stating 'If you seek his monument look around.'

As their revenue increased, the dippers placed advertisements in newspapers, such as the *Lewes Journal* (Lewes, the county town, was just seven miles away). On 3rd April 1780, we read:

BRIGHTHELMSTON. SEA BATHING
This is to acquaint the Nobility, Gentry and others, resorting to Brighthelmston, that MARTHA TUTT, MARY GUILDFORD, SUSANNAH GUILDFORD, ELIZABETH WINGHAM, and ANN SMITH, five strong Women, all used to the Sea, have completely fitted up a set of NEW MACHINES, with a Careful Man and Horse, to conduct them in and out of the Water, for the purpose of BATHING LADIES AND CHILDREN, the Ladies at One Shilling each, and Children Sixpence. Attendance will be given every morning.

N.B. Orders received at THE RISING SUN near the bathing.

The Rising Sun was an inn near the end of East Street. It has a terrific ghost story, related later.

Two great Brighton characters emerged during these dipping years. One was John

Dipper Martha Gunn

10

'Smoaker' Miles, the other was Martha Gunn.

Smoaker was the chief dipper for men, Martha for women, as bathing was strictly segregated, with one beach area for women, one for men – and a great big space in between! A little ditty, about these two, ran:

Smoaker Miles

> There's plenty of dippers and jokers,
> And salt-water rigs for your fun;
> The King of them all is Old Smoaker,
> The Queen of them all, Martha Gunn.

Two amusing stories about the pair are told a bit

Bathing machines at Brighthelmstone, 1788

11

The Prince of Wales comes to town

further on. Of course, there would occasionally be the odd person who didn't bathe using a machine. In August 1805, the *Morning Herald* contained the following Brighton news item:

> The greatest novelty that this part of the coast exhibited this morning, was a Gentleman undressing himself on the Beach, for the purpose of a ducking, in front of the town, attended by his lady, who 'sans difference', supplied him with napkins, and even assisted him in wiping the humid effects of his exercise from his brawny limbs, as he returned from the water to dress.'

Such an incident would have been the talk of the town!

ROYAL PATRONAGE

Fortunately for Brighton, as interest in seawater bathing was reaching fever pitch and more and more facilities were being laid on for the droves of fashionable visitors coming to the town, the dice of circumstance rolled as never before in the town's favour. For who should come a-calling at Brighton in 1783, but the heir to the throne of England, George Frederick Augustus, the Prince of Wales, later King George IV.

The Prince, aged twenty-one, had come to visit his uncle, the wonderfully scurrilous Duke of Cumberland, famous for all sorts of scandalous behaviour, such as in 1770, having to pay £10,000 in damages for seducing the wife of a notable lord (it was quite legal to seek damages for this 'offence' then). The Prince liked Brighton and on a second visit was advised to try the sea-water cure to relieve glandular swellings he had in his throat. He was suitably dipped and seemed to benefit. There's a nice story of a later bathing session with Smoaker Miles who found the Prince swimming away from him, just a little too far for comfort. Rather than politely requesting his charge to return, Smoaker caught him by the ear and dragged him back to his machine, like a naughty boy, fearing he'd have the death of the heir to the throne on his hands if he weren't more vigilant!

The Prince took a real liking to Brighton and whimsically decided to live in the town whenever the fancy took him. A clerk found a suitable house for him in 1786, just beyond East Street, that would subsequently be altered and enlarged many times (again, whenever the fancy took him), to become Brighton's famous Royal

The Steine, Royal Pavilion and The Dome in 1806

13

Pavilion. Some enlarging! The final version of the building, which was completed in 1823, was conceived as an oriental fantasy by John Nash and cost the then astronomic sum of more than £500,000 to create. Close by, between 1803 and 1808, he had a huge, circular stable built to house his horses and carriages (today, the Dome concert hall), plus an extensive riding school (the Corn Exchange).

With an eligible royal resident in town and the wealthy and fashionable following at his heels – in the cartoon on page 12, they're portrayed as donkeys – Brighton's popularity went through the roof. The population in 1780 had been just 3,800 people. In 1831, it would be 40,5000.

> If you're sick of the earth,
> Take a twelve-shilling berth,
> On the roof of the fast coach, the Triton.
> In five hours and a half,
> You shall sing dance and laugh,
> In this Mahomet's paradise – Brighton!'

So ran another ditty of the period. All manner of amenities began appearing for the amusement and diversion of these visitors, including fine new hotels, indoor bath buildings (so dipping could carry on even in bad weather), ballrooms, a racecourse, library and theatre. The town also expanded physically, in a huge way, to accommodate new residents, with street after street of small tenements being built up, mainly to the east of the town, to house the servants, tradesmen and small workshop premises the place now needed (saddle and harness makers seemed to do particularly well). High class, exclusive crescents and squares were built at the eastern and western extremities of the town, to house the really wealthy who wanted to reside in Brighton permanently, but 'out of town', on its fringes, away from the central noise and bustle.

But returning to the seafront a while longer. Some lovely insights into life on Brighton's beaches in the 1820s are given in the memoirs of Maud Egerton King, whose father ran one of the coaching offices in the town then, when she was just a child. By now, George, Prince of Wales had become King George IV of England and his Pavilion was more or less finished:

In the foreground of this old Brighton lay the beach full of the quaint life and business of the fishery folk. Down came the beaux and butterflies who were guests at the Pavilion, and sometimes the King himself. The burly fishermen accepted the petting at the patronising with amused toleration; they taught the gentlemen to swim and grinned at their first flounderings; and they spoke of their anointed sovereign as 'Jarge'. The daintiest ladies delivered themselves delightedly into the hands of the fat bathing women in their short petticoats, and, were they duchesses or daughters of half-pay captains, submitted merrily to their duckings and dousings and accepted as part of this charming topsy-turvy life by the sea

Fisherman of the period

that the old creatures should scold them for their venturesomeness and hail each of them as, 'my dear'.

Old Master Hurst and his three sons (giants in size and strength were all four of them) had saved more lives, it was said, than any other ten on Brighton beach; but if you questioned them on the matter they were as shy as children, and did you press them to relate but one of their stirring adventures, would invariably ask you, had you ever heard of their grandmother, old Mis' Hurst, who was reported the strongest woman 'long all the coast in her time; for by simply sitting down and pulling at a rope with her heels dug into the sand, she could haul up a boat as well as any capstan.

'How many did ye say there was of them father?' roared Tim Hurst when, at our earnest request, he took us into his rope-shop to show us his greatest treasure. This was a testimonial presented to his father and brothers by a number of persons they had rescued from a wreck one bitter night – a large roll of parchment, whereon were the signatures of those saved, surmounted by a deal of handsome and totally illegible blazoning in red, blue and gold.

'Thirt'-nine and a dog,' said old master Hurst, who was smoking with closed eyes in the sun outside.

'Well I say forty and a dog,' roared Tim again.

'Thirt'-nine's the figger I tell ye boy,' growled the old giant, opening one eye and peering in at us; 'and don't go pilin' up reckonings in that way, or mebbe th' Almighty won't let ye do the like again.'

MRS FITZHERBERT

But back to the 'main plot' of this part of the guide again, when George Frederick Augustus was still Prince of Wales and heir to the throne. There followed for him, starting in the 1780s, a passionate love affair with a woman named Maria Fitzherbert, with whom he became madly (to put it mildly) infatuated, in an amazing 'on and off' fashion for virtually the rest of his life. Take a big, deep breath for what follows.

Maria Fitzherbert was twenty-eight when the Prince first met her at the theatre in London. She was twice widowed; her first husband died from falling off his horse, the second from a chill. She was refined and beautiful, utterly dazzling the Prince, who was just twenty-two years old. The pursuit he then instigated, to woo her and win her love, was as if he'd gone mad; he spent thousands of

George and Maria chained in love

pounds buying jewellery and other gifts for her and he even feigned a suicide attempt, by stabbing (more like pricking) himself with a blade of some kind and obtaining the necessary gore from squeezing leeches. But it worked and she agreed to marry him, the only problem being it would be completely illegal because she was not an approved choice and also she was a Roman Catholic; the Prince, on becoming king, would become head of the Church of England. So what to do? Secretly marry of course, which they did, in the drawing room of her London home, in 1785. The only clergyman the Prince could find to perform the ceremony was in the Fleet Prison, London, for being in debt. This was a man named John Burt, who received £500 for performing the ceremony. Only five people were present, two of them signing the marriage certificate, which the Prince wrote out himself. Did the Prince tell his father, King George III, what he'd done? Of course he didn't! Later, as rumours grew, the marriage had to be officially denied in Parliament – several times.

The Prince and 'Mrs Prince' (as Martha Gunn called her), stayed in Brighton during the summer months, returning to London each winter. As the marriage was secret (but everyone knew about it), they occupied different houses; he lodged in the Pavilion and she lived in property close by. Later she lived in Old Steine, at Steine House, which still exists and is described more fully later on. The Prince often appeared on the balcony there, with a smile on his face, but no one ever saw him leave the Pavilion, leading to speculation there was a secret tunnel between his place and hers. More speculation about them having children has only recently been confirmed. There were seven offspring altogether and they managed to live a completely separate life with them in the countryside among the gentry, passing off as the Payne family. Only in her lifetime did the youngest daughter, Minney, strongly hint that George was her father. A Roman Catholic register of baptisms in Brighton was begun in 1799 just before her birth. Several early pages in this have been sliced out - supposedly part of the secrecy plot.

George never had it in him to be faithful to any one woman and he had an affair with an actress named Anna Maria Crouch in the early 1790s. He returned to Maria though, and seemed happy and settled with her, but as the years slipped by, it was clear a proper, legal wife would have to be found for the young heir to the throne, and for some offspring to be produced to succeed him. Caroline of Brunswick (a cousin, from Germany) was accordingly produced to become the official wife, marrying the Prince in 1795, purely for political reasons and so he could get more money from Parliament

Queen Caroline with Princess Charlotte

to clear his vast debts (he had no idea of the value of money throughout his entire life; in 1792 it's known he was £370,000 in debt). In 1794 the fickle Prince abruptly ended his relationship with Mrs Fitzherbert by a simple, blunt letter, informing her it was over. This wasn't just because he was about to marry officially – although he was – it was also because he was having another affair, this time with Lady Jersey, a grandmother of forty. Getting complicated isn't it?

Queen Caroline was (how can we put this?) a coarse, unhygienic German whom the Prince hated. The day of his wedding, George was so drunk (on brandy apparently) he had to be 'assisted' up the

aisle and was so repulsed by his new bride he is said to have spent his honeymoon night in a fireplace. She deserves quite a bit of sympathy though as the Prince was generally pretty horrible to her whenever he could be. Once, he received a message stating, 'Your worst enemy is dead'. He's supposed to have replied, quite calmly, 'Oh, is she?'

However, they consummated the marriage very rapidly and a daughter – Princess Charlotte – was born to them, nine months after the wedding, in 1796. With the succession to the throne seem-

In the Saloon at the Marine Pavilion, 1788

ingly secure, the Prince and Caroline immediately separated. When news of this got out, the outrage was so vociferous, the Prince spent the 1796 season hiding further along the coast at Bognor to avoid the flak. If their daughter hadn't died in child-birth, in 1817, the country would have had a Queen Charlotte instead of Queen Victoria.

The main reason for the separation, other than the fact the Prince could not stand Caroline, was that his passion for Mrs Fitzherbert had flared up again and he pleaded (oh, how he pleaded!) for a reunion. He even altered his will leaving everything to her and had the Pope (no less) declare that Maria was his true wife in the eyes of God. And he threatened suicide again. It took several years for her to capitulate, but eventually, in 1799, they were reconciled. He'd 'dumped' (to use modern parlance) Lady Jersey by now, although, due to her wily nature, she had somehow secured for herself the job of lady-in-waiting to poor old Queen Caroline and she was pretty horrible to her too. We're told that for Maria the years that followed 'were the happiest of her connection with the

Prince' and she herself told Lord Stourton that they were 'extremely poor, but as merry as crickets'. But fickle fellow that he was, the Prince had yet another affair, this time with Lady Hertford, and finally parted company with Maria in 1811 in a seemingly, quite reasonable way. They met occasionally, at various functions, but that was about it.

But another crisis was brewing which clearly distracted the Prince from affairs of the heart. By now, his father, King George III, was unfit to rule and people thought he was going mad. He probably had the condition known as porphyria, a metabolism problem, which can result in delirium. Anyway, a Parliamentary Bill was passed, making the Prince's title that of Regent, which meant he was now ruler of the country, even though the King still lived. Power must have made him go a bit soft in the head too, for in 1820, he had Caroline put on trial for – of all things – adultery! Parliament wisely withdrew the charge. The Prince was finally crowned King George IV in 1821 (he had Caroline locked out of the coronation ceremony); he was monarch for just ten years. But his epic love story with Mrs Fitzherbert must have its 'ahhh' ending of course, and it does. George was sixty-seven when he died. The Duke of Wellington found a locket on his body, as it lay in the open coffin. It contained a miniature portrait of, guess who? Yes, it was of Maria – the real love of his life – and it was duly buried with him. She had a matching locket containing George's portrait, which she left in her will to Minney.

Mrs Fitzherbert, who must be one of the most stoic, forgiving and patient women ever seduced by royalty, died in Brighton, in 1837, aged eighty. She was buried in a Roman Catholic church to the east of the town (St John the Baptist, out of the area covered by this guide), where her memorial has her wearing three wedding rings. Phew!

BRIGHTON 1788-1820

The late 1700s, through to the time of George IV's coronation in 1820, is easily the most fascinating and scandalous time in Brighton's history (and all the above was just a taster!), and one of the main reasons for its enduring fascination among visitors and residents alike. These years are loosely termed the Regency period, which really was from 1811, when the Prince officially took over from his deranged father, until becoming King himself nine years later. Often though, it's said to start from George III's first period of 'madness' in 1788. This guide goes along with that and now details the main features of the Regency period, which can be skipped if the reader wants to get on to more modern times in Brighton (if so, jump on a few pages to The Coming Of The Railway on page 29).

Another big breath needed! The Regency period was, as we've just seen, a strange and heady mix of elegance, taste and debauchery. For the wealthy in Brighton, as in other key towns and cities of the period, social gatherings, balls, soirees and card schools were conducted in an atmosphere of great refinement and gentility, with everyone bowing and scraping, but masking a prodigious preoccupation with scandal, sex and indulgence. And you can imagine the whispers that went round Brighton's fashionable meeting places when the Prince's love life took another turn or two.

An outrageous gossip writer of these times, known as Anthony Pasquin (who probably didn't dare write using his real name, John Williams), published *The New Brighton Guide* in 1796, and in it he sent up the social scene of the time, offering disgraceful – but very funny – advice for both ladies and gentlemen 'of distinction', on how best to be noticed when visiting Brighton. This is what his guide advised, for young ladies when attending the theatre:

> We recommend to them, to make as much noise and as great a flutter as will be borne, upon their entering the boxes in a theatre; this is perfectly fashionable and will assuredly make them stared at by the vulgar order of the audience, who dare not imitate them in their low sphere. If they cannot attract attention by laughing, talking in a high key, or abrupt gesticulations with the fan, we recommend them to drop their cloak or shawl, as by accident, into the pit. If the cloak should be caught in its declension by a chandelier and publicly burned, it will prove uncommonly interesting and charming and will probably be mentioned in all the newspapers.

He advised ladies to:

> Seize every decent pretence to expose the charms of the neck and the bosom; this is satisfying the curiosity of admiration; and to render those comfortable who are around us, is one of the first principles of good breeding. We recommend to them, to be the first in getting into a carriage, if there be men in company, that they may have a complete occasion of showing a well turned ankle to the searching eyes of the accompanying beaus, who will not fail to communicate to all they know, as a great secret, that Miss Such-a-one has a damned handsome leg. This is a sure trap to win a lover but not a husband; but as husbands are so seldom lovers, that is not much to be regretted.

The guide advises men to:

> Reel into the theatre during the performance in a state of assumed intoxication, and be sure to disturb the audience in the most interesting part of the drama, by taking liberties with any who harbour in the green boxes (in other words, young ladies)

Evening Party in the Pavilion's Yellow Room

and are unhappily devoted to insult; by this manoeuvre, if dexterously managed, they will gain three important points: the first is, the credit of having consumed more wine than their income will allow; the second is a disposition for unlimited intrigue; and the third is an opportunity of displaying their contempt of good manners without any hazard of personal danger.

Pasquin's guide contains pages of this sort of stuff, in thoroughly bad taste, but his book was reprinted six times (at least), so must have been widely read, if not acted on, at the turn of the eighteenth century in Brighton.

Yet it was symptomatic of the Regency period that it produced the poet Lord Byron and writer Jane Austen (both admired by the Prince) and also that virtuoso dandy, Beau Brummel, the last word in taste and fashion, who introduced the stylish, stiffened cravats that the best-dressed gentlemen of the period wore, including the Prince of Wales himself (who was a friend of Brummel). While John Nash (designer of the Pavilion) was glorifying London with classically arcaded buildings, Thomas Hope published his definitive treatise *Household Furniture and Decorative Arts*, extolling the virtues of incorporating Egyptian and Greek motifs into interior design, and the great cream-coloured Regency crescents, squares and terraced housing rose up in various parts of Britain, giving breathtaking style and elegance to places like Brighton, Bath and Cheltenham.

But what about life at the Pavilion during these years? The time it metamorphosed from farmhouse to classical villa, then to oriental Pavilion. Was it wine, women and song all the way? Were drunkenness, gambling and hanky-panky taking place all the time? You bet your life they were! Well, a lot of the time anyway. There are tales of Charles Howard, the eleventh Duke of Norfolk, becoming so utterly intoxicated while dining at the Pavilion, he was carried out on a stretcher (by four footmen, showing 'a dexterity that betrayed long practice') with hardly anyone batting an eyelid. Dining lasted from four to six hours then, usually followed by gambling, and the Pavilion had a special room, permanently fitted up, where guests could 'retire' to indulge in betting games.

And sex? Well, intelligence (as it was called then) is a bit scanty, but Anthony Pasquin hints in his guide at what was going on, when advising visitors where to stay in the town:

> There are lodgings for £20 per week on the cliffs to half a crown per night in a stable; and the sinews of morality are so happily relaxed that a bawd and a baroness may snore in the same happy tenement.'

I think we get the picture.

One of the most amusing incidents at the Pavilion took place when a grand ball was in progress and the Prince, probably a bit bored, went into a side room with some ladies and started showing off his skills with a small rifle. He shot at a target placed across the room, then offered the weapon to the ladies to try. One shot a hole in the door, another disfigured the ceiling, and then Lady Downshire promptly discharged it through an open door and shot a violinist playing in the orchestra!

Another good story concerns Martha Gunn, the bathing woman, who was friendly with the Prince and had access to the Pavilion kitchens. On one occasion, he saw her slip a packet of butter into her pocket when she thought no one was looking. He started chatting to her and drew her gradually towards the huge fireplace, where, after a short while, the butter melted and dribbled down her clothes, revealing her kleptomania. He was probably very amused by the incident.

The Prince kept some thoroughly bad company during his time in Brighton, most notably with three youths from an aristocratic family named Barrymore. These young men (and they had a sister too, who swore, it's said, like a fish seller) were of Irish descent, amazingly rich and thoroughly decadent. As boys (left without parents from an early age) they had gone out one night with carpenters' tools and changed all the inn signs around in the area where they lived. Arriving in Brighton in 1788, when the eldest, Richard – the seventh Earl – was just twenty-years-old, they idled away their time getting up to all sorts of mischief and taking part in silly contests, betting huge sums they could complete any challenge set them. Every wager to do with horses was immediately taken up as Richard was a skilled horseman and could often be found racing other coaches round the Steine. The Prince of Wales frequently kept their company (he liked all this messing about too) and he once came hurrying out of the Pavilion to act as referee in a fight Richard had picked with a man named Fox, whose father, so he thought, had insulted him in a newspaper article.

Black Lion Lane

People sometimes got the better of 'the Barrys' though, such as when Richard was challenged by a man named Bullock to a running race. This seemed no contest – Bullock was huge and portly; he could be beaten even if it were a walking race. But Bullock stipulated, as part of the wager, that he could choose the course and be allowed a ten-yard start. Barrymore readily agreed and the Prince came over from the Pavilion to watch. Bullock cunningly chose one of the narrowest passages in the town for the race, Black Lion Lane (this still exists, described later), and being hemmed in by walls all the way along, Barrymore just couldn't pass Bullock, so lost.

Another time saw Henry Barrymore (the second brother, who became the eighth earl) challenged to a duel on the Steine, following a dispute in a card game, which he duly accepted. His opponent was a stout and elderly Member of Parliament named Howarth. They met at five in the morning, and on taking their places, pistols ready, Howarth calmly began removing his clothes, until he stood facing his opponent in just his drawers. He said he had been a doctor once and learnt the importance of keeping a wound clean! Some shots were fired but the incident seems to have ended good-humouredly.

The most outrageous wager was when the Duke of Bedford bet Richard he could produce a man who would eat a cat alive, in front of them – all of it. He went out and tried to induce some person or other to do the act, offering huge payment, but without success. So another bet was lost.

Even Mrs Fitzherbert wasn't spared a jolly jape or two. Henry Barrymore was bet he couldn't ride a horse all the way up the stairs of her house in the Steine (pictured left). This was duly attempted, but having reached the top floor the animal refused to descend, so blacksmiths had to be sent for to 'persuade' it down. Mrs Fitzherbert, we learn, was very amused by the incident.

The Barrys delighted, too, in shocking residents and visitors by outrageous jokes and behaviour, which they thought terribly funny. One bit of fun was to prop an open coffin upright, complete with dummy corpse, against someone's front door (at night), ring the bell, then hide to enjoy what followed. Whoever opened the door would have the corpse flop down into the house causing, no doubt, screams of consternation from any ladies and probably making one or two to faint (which was the idea of course). They did this too with a servant playing the corpse, suitably dressed and covered with white powder, who would step out of the coffin and stagger into the house scaring everyone witless. On one occasion the footman was shot at.

Steine House staircase

All this buffoonery clearly affected the general staidness of the town; we learn that the use of the stocks was so stretched for drunken behaviour that often, 'there being but four holes, one leg alone of each delinquent was secured'.

And we wonder at the antics of today's youth!

Yet by the time the Prince had become George IV, in 1820, he seemed to tire of all this jollity and, sadly, of Brighton itself. Perhaps he'd just run out of energy, as he'd grown extremely fat by now.

His still evolving seaside home, the Royal Pavilion, would

The Barrymores' corpse at the door

become a real case of 'after you get what you want you don't want it' as, between 1821 and his death in 1830, he visited the place only three more times. When he died he was pretty much disliked by his subjects and was succeeded by William IV, who they liked a lot better. He in turn was followed by niece Queen Victoria, who again was popular, but she didn't like Brighton and her predecessor's Pavilion, because she couldn't see the sea from it, everyone was far too nosey and wouldn't leave her alone. So, needing money to rebuild Buckingham Palace in London, she sold the Pavilion to the town of Brighton, in 1850, and it was soon converted into the tourist attraction it is today.

And the rest of this guide is going to seem a bit dull after that lot!

King William IV

Queen Victoria

GEORGE IV's SUCCESSORS

William IV stayed at the Pavilion at least once every year of his reign. Servants and friends thought he was virtually teetotal compared with George IV, as he drank only a pint of sherry with his dinner. He was also delightfully quirky; once, at a New Year's Eve ball, his dancing partner was a sixty-one year old admiral! He didn't share his brother's interest in architecture or the decorative arts, saying all that sort of thing was just 'knick-knackery'. William had ten children, all by an actress named Dora Jordan, but none by his wife, so his niece became Queen in 1837. Victoria also used the Royal Pavilion as a seaside residence, but, as already said, found the early railway trippers tiresome, and gave up the Pavilion for the peace of Osborne House on the Isle of Wight.

Victoria removed all the furniture and fittings from the Pavilion (143 vans took the contents away between 1847 and 1848) and the Commissioners of Brighton, forerunner of the council, bought it from her in 1850 more or less as an empty shell. Refurbished and restored, with many items on permanent loan from the present Queen, Elizabeth II, the Pavilion has been a top tourist attraction ever since and an absolute 'must see' for any visitor to Brighton and Hove. Here, the self-indulgent atmosphere of the 1820s is so marvellously intact, particularly inside the breathtaking banqueting hall, that you half expect the Prince to be there, seated at the head of the table, stuffing himself with yet another course from the menu that's on show and ogling the bosom of some wench perched on his knee.

Queen Victoria's son, Edward VII (Bertie) often came to Brighton, where he stayed with his daughter, the Duchess of Fife, or his millionaire friends, the Sassoons, in their house on the seafront at Hove. Subsequent royal visits have been much more intermittent and no king or queen has ever stayed in Brighton the way George IV, William IV and Queen Victoria did.

King Edward VII

THE COMING OF THE RAILWAY

When London trains reached Brighton for the first time in 1841, early in Queen Victoria's reign, the town boomed all over again. Now 'trippers' poured into Brighton, mainly from London, and there began a new wave of prosperity which lasted right through to the 1930s. A ditty of this period ran:

> I took the train to Brighton – I walked beside the sea,
> And thirty thousand Londoners were there along with me.
> We crowded every lodging, and we lumbered each hotel,
> Sniffed the briny for an appetite, and dined extremely well.

Many of these new visitors had never been to the seaside before. The town mushroomed again, and a large number of attractions

The Aquarium in 1894

The opening of Magnus Volk's Electric Railway, 1883

and new hotels were built as amenities for this influx of trippers, including the West Pier (1866), the Aquarium (1872 – now a SeaLife centre) and Volk's Electric Railway (1883), all of which still exist today (in the case of the West Pier, only just, following years of decay and a partial collapse in January 2003).

THE WAR YEARS AND BETWEEN

At present, historians are tending to see the two world wars as one thirty-year conflict, with a brief, somewhat fragile peace in between. World War I was fought 'over there' in the fields of northern France and Belgium between 1914 and 1918, and was principally a European war, with Britain, France and Russia as allies against Germany, Italy and Austria-Hungary. Essentially, it was a conflict that flared up following massive disputes about possession of land. Britain was not invaded, but the sounds of shelling could be heard from the hills around Brighton and one huge detonation of shells was even heard in London.

Many Brighton buildings served as military hospitals during World War I, due to the town's close proximity to the battlefields of France. Bizarrely, the Royal Pavilion became a hospital for Indians, at the King's request. He believed that these 'men of the Empire', would be at ease in the Indian-style surroundings of the building. Stories of unconscious Indians reviving and believing they were in heaven because of the sumptuous décor, are quite true.

The period between the wars, the 1920s and 1930s, is when Brighton peaked in popularity, and those who lived then have spoken and written of its dance halls, cinemas, cheap public transport (electric trams), clean sea to bathe in, flourishing piers, the electrification of the railway and any number of new amenities opening including swimming pools, cinemas, an ice rink, several parks and new schools. The town expanded enormously in 1928, taking in outlying places and areas of land, becoming five times the size it was previously. Such was the confidence, civic pride and municipal vision generated during this period, there were even mind-boggling plans to rebuild the entire seafront – from one end to the

Trams at Old Steine

other – in Art Deco style, championed by a wealthy and dynamic councillor, Herbert Carden, known as the 'father of modern Brighton'.

The 1920s and 1930s were Brighton's golden years and many a pensioner will recall misspending his or her youth at places like the Regent Dance Hall, Sherry's (mentioned later) and the town's numerous theatres and cinemas. The West

Dancing at the Regent Ballroom in the 1920s

The West Pier, about 1930

Pier received the highest number of visitors ever in 1920 – 2,074,000 people. But what brought these glory days to an end was World War II, from 1939 to 1945. This war, again against Germany and its allies, was completely different from the 1914-1918 one; it was a far more widespread conflict and many European countries were overrun and occupied. Britain was heavily bombed and Brighton was attacked by German aircraft fifty-six times between 1940 and 1944. One hundred and ninety-eight people were killed, 357 seriously injured, and

433 slightly injured. Being a prominent town on the south coast, Brighton prepared for the possibility of an invasion force landing on its beaches. The town was virtually closed down; it became a restricted area, had land mines hidden on its beaches and both piers were cut in half, so they couldn't act as landing stages for enemy ships. It was only the Battle of Britain, where the Royal Air Force destroyed enemy aircraft time and time again in dog fights above the skies of southern Britain, that made the German leader, Adolf Hitler, postpone the invasion of Britain in Operation Sealion. It's known though, that had he succeeded, the Royal Pavilion would have become his headquarters in the south of England.

POSTWAR BRIGHTON

The period immediately after World War II saw Brighton, as a bucket-and-spade holiday resort, in decline. In the late 1940s, the town received only 60 per cent of the visitors it had in the late 1930s and never really recovered its former image. The reasons for this are complex and had little to do with cheaper holidays abroad becoming available, or the rise of alternative types of holiday at home, such as camping or going to holiday camps.These didn't boom until the 1950s. The period immediately after World War II

High rise flats go up on Albion Hill

was a time of huge uncertainty and loss of direction. If people had money, they held on to it, as going on holiday seemed, for many families, sheer extravagance.

The 1960s and 1970s saw Brighton's heritage and history plundered, when the architectural answer to everything was high-rise and box-type buildings – which rose here, there and everywhere. These were sterile, dull years for the town, when some appalling things were built in the name of progress; many of them still have to be lived with. By the 1970s, it was thought Brighton needed a new direction, so there was heavy investment in the conference trade. The Brighton Centre, a multi-purpose entertainment building, went up in the mid-1970s. Sadly, the design of this was another graph-paper box, made worse by directly adjoining the delightfully light and Italianate Grand Hotel.

MODERN BRIGHTON AND HOVE

Brighton and the neighbouring town of Hove combined as one administrative authority in April 1987. This was after years of resistance to the idea, with many of the powers-that-be thinking genteel Hove would somehow be 'contaminated' by raffish Brighton. Once joined, a bid was made for city status, which was duly granted in December 2000.

Today Brighton is a place where literally anything goes. It's quite a sleazy city but at heart it's the unique and charismatic blend of culture and cockles it was 200 years ago. Something of the naughty reputation it achieved in the Regency period remains. It's probably true to say Brighton and Hove has become a 'twenty-something' city, with trendy pubs, clubs and discos flourishing for this age group, and some areas of Brighton are more alive at night than they are during the day. A three-week arts festival each May is second only to the Edinburgh Festival.

Brighton and Hove has all the social ills of most other cities in Britain, including homelessness (some forty people sleep rough on the streets each night), begging, drugs, crime, refuse problems and traffic problems, but this guide isn't about the city's present shortcomings. Details now follow of its three most ancient thoroughfares, East, West and North Streets (see map).

EAST STREET

Jervoise encounters Strike-a-light

This is Brighton's oldest street and could have existed as a cluster of dwellings back in Saxon times, with no name at all, and with a river running east of it, later called the Wellesbourne, which is still around, but flows underground. By the fourteenth century East Street would have been a proper street, although extremely narrow (it's still pretty narrow today) lined with tiny fishermen's cottages similar to others built right down on the beach at the foot of the cliffs. The change to a shopping thorough-fare came much later, in the wake of the Prince of Wales' visits and fashionable society wanting to buy goods from high-class shops. Great East Street, as it then was called, was much longer and ran past the Pavilion, which the heir to the throne did not like one bit, as people could peer through his windows.

East Street can claim Brighton's best ghost story, a real shocker, which took place in an inn on the eastern side of the street, near the seafront end, called the Rising Sun (demolished in the 1860s). A suitably stormy night on Brighton beach, about 1760, kicks the story off, when local fisherman Swan Jervoise was bringing his boat ashore with a good catch of herring. He noticed some brilliant flashes coming from windows of the Rising Sun, which should have been closed, so while his crew dealt with the boat and fish, he made his way to the inn to investigate. At the door he heard striking noises, flint against steel, like a tinderbox being used, only far louder, and the great flashes were coming through the win-dows and lighting up the street. He hammered on the door, expecting the landlord, whom he knew, to open it and explain what was going on. Instead, the door swept back revealing a monstrous, seven-foot tall apparition, with staring grey eyes set in a white face. The figure wore a black cloak and a tall, white, conical hat. This was the ghost known as Strike-a-light, who swept past Jervoise, out into East Street and was lost in the night.

The fisherman yelled hysterically, rousing the landlord, who sat Jervoise by the still-glowing fire and gave him some ale. Left alone, he was just starting to recover his wits, when he felt a presence in the room. Turning, he was appalled to find the ghastly, towering creature had returned and was pointing fixedly at the fire with a bony finger. Jervoise fainted, was found by the landlord and put to bed. A priest, Father Anselm, called the next day to minister to Jervoise, and was told how the spectre's gaze was focused on the fireplace. Jervoise then slumped back and died. The fireplace was duly searched and the hearthstone prised up. Underneath was found a hoard of treasure – a huge number of gold coins. This caused excavations to be made in the inn's ancient cellars (in case there was any more to be found), but only some old bones were unearthed, along with an ancient sword. The bones were reburied in the local churchyard, whereupon no more was heard of Strike-a-light, his apparent mission, to alert someone to the treasure's hiding place, finally achieved. What happened to the treasure? Some say it went to a priory in Lewes, others that it went to France.

From spooks to stationery. It's always claimed that a stationer in East Street, a man named Brewer, invented the humble envelope about 1830. This is a Brighton legend that can't be true as envelopes were being used in France in the 1690s, but Brewer may have been first to offer them to the general public in England and in various sizes too.

East Street today is still full of trendy shops and pubs but should have been fully pedestrianised years ago. Street entertainment often takes place here during the summer months. At the northern end is a taxi rank and opposite this, across Castle Square, is the gateway to Brighton's Royal Pavilion, but more about this later.

WEST STREET

West Street was the next street to appear during Brighton's forma-tive years, giving the town a new western boundary. The space between the streets became a place for growing hemp (now The Lanes), a plant made up of stringy fibres, used to make ropes.

There are no buildings of great antiquity in West Street any more except the bow-fronted restaurant near the bottom, on the eastern side, dating from about 1805.

The most famous incident to take place in the West Street of old involved a fleeting visit by Charles II. His father, Charles I, had lost the Civil War and been executed, by order of Parliament, in 1649. He had

Charles II

believed in 'the divine right of kings' by which he considered he had God-given power to rule as he thought best and Parliament should follow his dictates. His son, another Charles, continued to engage the Parliamentarians in skirmishes, but on losing the

The Royal Surprise

Battle of Worcester in 1651 had to flee the country (after famously hiding in an oak tree), so made his way to the south coast and Brighton.

At the George Inn the fugitive king met ship-owner Nicholas Tettersell, who took him to exile in France, via Shoreham (a town further west), in his brig *The Surprise*. The country was ruled by Parliament's champion, Oliver Cromwell, then by Cromwell's

38

son, but there was a wave of reaction against their rule – they adopted Puritan ideals, closing pubs and theatres, and banning Christmas from being celebrated. Charles was recalled and reinstated as king and all was forgiven (well, almost). Tettersell sailed up the River Thames in London to meet the King at Whitehall and claim some recompense for his efforts. He renamed his brig *The Royal Surprise* and was given a reward plus a post in the navy. But something went awry here and he resigned his post, becoming High Constable of Brighton in 1670. His years in this job are remembered only for the foul way he treated local Quakers. He died in 1674 and is buried in the churchyard of St Nicholas, where his tombstone eulogises his virtues. The George Inn, where he met the fleeing king, has long since gone, and on the site today is the tall hotel on the western side of West Street, next to the cinema.

Opposite, on the other side of the street, where a nightclub stands, stood a large house, bought by a man named Henry Thrale in 1767. This was when West Street was described as being at the 'court end of the town' (in other words, posh and select). Thrale and his wife, Hester, entertained the literary and artistic glitterati of the day at this house, including Fanny Burney, the diarist, playwright Oliver Goldsmith, Sir Joshua Reynolds, the painter and,

Thrale's house in West Street

The remaining post from the Thrales' house and a plaque marking the site of the building

most famous of all, the tetchy Dr Samuel Johnson, compiler of Britain's first anecdotal dictionary.

Getting Johnson to stay at Brighton for any length of time was a near miracle as he hated the place, although he did enjoy riding through the Sussex countryside. He found Brighton – a famous quote – 'so desolate, that if one had a mind to hang one's self for desperation at being obliged to live there, it would be difficult to find a tree on which to fasten a rope'.

The Thrale's house was demolished in 1866 and a large concert hall built on the site. This was a multi-purpose building and the Victorians' zeal for education saw many famous people of the day giving lectures here, including H M Stanley (of 'Dr Livingstone, I presume?' fame) and the

Dr Samuel Johnson

surgeon Frederick Treves, celebrated for his rescue of John Merrick (the 'Elephant Man').

The concert hall had a long and chequered history and was one of the first places in Brighton to show moving pictures in about 1902. It became the legendary dance hall Sherrys in 1919, which featured in Graham Greene's book *Brighton Rock*. Sherrys closed in 1948 and the building served as a bingo hall, then a roller-skating rink, before the frontage was rebuilt and the interior altered to make the building the modern nightclub it is today. Outside, one post from the Thrale's house, of over two hundred years ago, still stands (by a miracle) and is probably the oldest part of West Street remaining.

A famous duel was fought in West Street (the lower part, near the seafront) about 1770. This was between a Dr Kipping and 'an Officer' who had insulted him. Here, instead of wounding his opponent, and honour being satisfied, Kipping skilfully managed to wrest the sword from his adversary's grasp, flick it into the air and catch it. Then he announced he would be keeping the officer's weapon for a week, a matter of far more serious disgrace, apparently, than if he'd received a cut.

The weirdest incident in West Street occurred when author Charles Dickens was staying at number 60 in 1849. The landlord of his lodgings quite suddenly went berserk for no accountable reason and ran amok. His daughter went mad too at exactly the same time. Understandably, Dickens fled to the Bedford Hotel on the seafront. What happened to the landlord and his daughter isn't known.

West Street contains a really fine church. This is St Paul's, on the western side, designed by a man named Carpenter and built between 1846 and 1847. The spire, unusually in wood, was added in the 1870s. The building was financed by the Reverend Henry Wagner, who, with his son, Arthur, paid for eleven of Brighton's churches to be built in the 1800s (mostly from their own pockets),

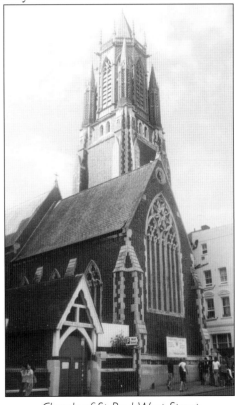

Church of St Paul, West Street

41

several of which are of national importance. Arthur Wagner became the permanent curate of St Paul's, and followed highly ritualistic ceremonies, which caused much concern among Church of England authorities who dubbed his methods 'Anglo-Catholicism'. Arthur Wagner caused huge controversy too when he refused to give evidence against a woman accused of

The Reverend Henry Wagner

murdering her brother. She had admitted her crime to Wagner in the confession box, but he would not repeat to the authorities what she had told him. He was assaulted in the street and even shot at, once the story became public. The woman, named Constance Kent, was subsequently found guilty and imprisoned.

NORTH STREET

If East Street was where all the fancy shops eventually existed, and West Street had most entertainment buildings over the years, then North Street has been the business street of the town, where most banks, building societies and insurance offices could be found at one time or another. Sadly, only a few historic buildings exist in the street today.

At the top of North Street, at the junction with West Street, stands Brighton's Clock Tower, unveiled in 1888, to commemorate Queen Victoria's Golden Jubilee the year before. Financed by a wealthy Brighton advertising magnate, James Willing, it stands seventy feet high and has recently been fully renovated, despite causing much derision as a piece of architecture over the years. 'Worthless', is how one writer summed up its merits.

Opposite the Clock Tower is a large branch of Boots the chemists, which dates from 1979. Before Boots, the site was occupied by the Regent Cinema, one of the first 'super-cinemas' built anywhere in Britain, opening in 1921 and lasting until 1973. There's information about this cinema on a wall inside the entrance (Queen's Road side).

Brighton's very first theatre stood in North Street, not far down from the Clock Tower, but on the southern side of the road. This operated for only a

The Regent Cinema

short period, 1774-1789, before moving to Duke Street (its story continues in that section). The shop now on the site has a relief medallion, on the

The head of Shakespeare?

second storey, of an 'Elizabethan' head. Is this of Shakespeare? Probably not, but it would be fitting if it were, being fixed to the location of the town's first proper theatre.

Much further down, on the other (northern) side, is a red

The Clock Tower, about 1910

43

Chapel Royal

brick church with a clock tower. This is the Chapel Royal, which was built between 1793 and 1795, when the town's main church, St Nicholas (just out of the area covered by this guide), had too many people wanting to attend, and a 'chapel of ease' was built to accommodate them. The Prince of Wales attended this chapel (virtually next door to the Pavilion), but walked out when he felt a particularly critical sermon on morals was aimed at him. The chapel was completely rebuilt in red brick, between 1877 and 1884; this is the building you see today. It still bears the Prince of Wales' coat of arms, just as the original had done, despite the famous walkout.

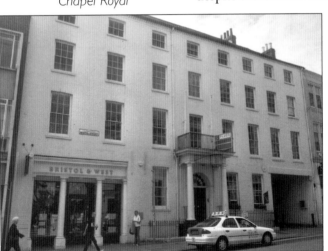

The old Clarence Hotel, North Street

Between the theatre site and the Chapel Royal, on the south side, about half way up, stands the most historic building to survive in North Street. Today it houses a building society, but in the past was a prosperous coaching hostelry, called the New Inn. It dates from 1785, and a description of it, in 1812, lists ten sitting rooms, twenty-six bedrooms, two kitchens, plus music, coffee and billiard rooms. The stabling could accommodate fifty horses and six coaches. It became the Clarence Hotel in 1830, the change of name coming from the new King, William IV, who formerly was the Duke of

The Theatre Royal

Clarence. It closed as a hotel as recently as 1972.

On the other side of the road from this building and slightly lower down is New Road. This is out of our area, but contains Brighton's Theatre Royal, a building that was two hundred years old in 2007. There isn't a famous actor or actress who hasn't appeared here over the years – Sean Connery, Diana Rigg, Michael Caine, Lauren Bacall, Marlene Dietrich, Charlton Heston, Laurence Olivier, Paul Scofield, Alec Guinness, Maggie Smith, Peter O'Toole, Edith Evans, Vincent Price, Noel Coward … just name anyone!

KING'S ROAD

Go down either West Street or East Street and you'll come to the southern boundary of the Old Town area, which is, naturally enough, the seafront road – King's Road – and its promenade and beaches. This road was opened by King George IV (hence its name) in 1822, after he contributed 200 guineas to its initial cost (a

The beach and cliffs in 1853

The Victorian arches of 1886

guinea being a pound and five pence in today's British money). As he rode along in his carriage at the opening ceremony, he was unexpectedly pelted with sugar-coated plums, according to an ancient custom, peculiar it seems to Sussex (even as late as the 1870s, sugar plums were strewn on paths leading to churches at weddings in the area).

There's a lot to take in on the seafront, and this part of the guide starts from the railings opposite the Old Ship Hotel. Before the laying out of King's Road and the proper development of the lower promenade, there were still bare chalk cliffs here, with the beach and sea below. Hard to imagine with today's traffic thundering past!

Railings were first installed along the cliff top in 1726 when, presumably, there was some kind of track in place, but certainly no proper road. Following King's Road being built, it was the coming of the railway to Brighton, in 1841, that slowly forced changes to the beach area and a proper promenade was formed in 1886. King's Road was then widened southwards, over the beach, on brick arches. These are still in place, housing most of the shops and amusements that make up the lower promenade of today. The railings directly above this promenade also date from 1886.

Facing the sea from opposite the Old Ship, the Brighton Pier, on the left (east), opened in 1899 as the Brighton Marine Palace and Pier. Then it was the third pier to be built in Brighton. This is overloaded with amusements and rides now, losing a fine theatre in 1983, where all manner of performers appeared over the years, including ballerina Anna Pavlova, Hermione Gingold, Julie Christie, Dick Emery and Ronnie Corbett. The last show here was in 1973.

To the west (on the right), is the wreck of the West Pier, which opened in 1866 and closed in 1975, due to lack of maintenance. It was designed by Eusebius Birch, who was also responsible for Brighton Aquarium.

After shutting down, it was made a Grade I listed building, then the only pier in the country granted this status. Many, many attempts were made to restore the pier and restore it to its former glory, but, none came off. This too had a theatre, from 1903, which saw performances from Charlie Chaplin,

The West Pier in 2002 prior to collapse and arson attacks

Stan Laurel, James Whale, Ellen Terry, Edith Evans, Rex Harrison, Ralph Richardson, Ronald Coleman and Robert Morley. It closed at the outbreak of World War II and was later converted into an amusement arcade.

The central concert hall collapsed in early 2002 and several arson attacks left the pier a burnt out wreck. To restore the pier, the cost was put at some £30 million, just to replace the piles, substructure and decking. Buildings and facilities on it would have pushed the final bill to an astronomical amount. Each new plan for restoration

Fishing Museum below King's Road

48

*The Old
Ship Hotel,
Brighton's
oldest*

seemed to generate controversy and as the years slip by and nothing's happened, the skeletal remains have become more and more dilapidated. A major collapse of what's left seems inevitable.

Below King's Road is the lower promenade of today, recently modernised in stages. A fish market operated here until 1960 and the hard, where catches were sold, can still be made out. There's a fine fishing museum, well worth a visit, where a good salty feel of how the beaches of Brighton once were can be genuinely felt. Ask any 'fishy' question you like of the friendly staff here and they'll have the answer. Stretching away either side of the museum are any number of shops selling drinks, seaside rock, ice creams, inflatable beach toys, shellfish and crab sticks, camera film, suntan lotion, postcards, etc. There are pubs, art and craft shops, amusements, sports courts, fairground rides and you might just find a fortune teller open for the season too, who'll tell you if you're to meet a tall dark stranger during your visit. The huge boomerang-shaped piece of metal between the piers, which many think part of a shipwreck or a washed-up submarine, is actually a sculpture.

Turning round and facing inland, still opposite the Old Ship Hotel, the seafront buildings here are a real mixture of old and new, with hardly any in their original, early 1800s form.

The Old Ship, the city's oldest hotel, dates back to the sixteenth century (but has been rebuilt since then, probably several times). It was an ancient coaching hostelry, also once used to hold meetings for town business and as a magistrates' court from time to time. In

1795 a court-martial was held here resulting in two militiamen receiving the death penalty for mutiny.

The Old Ship Hotel features in Thakeray's *Vanity Fair*, published (in serial form) in 1847. Thackeray wrote a large

The Grand Hotel

part of it while staying at the hotel, and made Brighton the town where his two main characters, George and Amelia, stay following their marriage. Charles Dickens was another literary guest.

After the IRA bomb

In 1831 the violinist Paganini performed in the hotel assembly rooms. He announced that his fee would be fifty guineas, which flabbergasted the promoter, but Paganini later took great delight in giving most of it back.

The most stylish hotel in King's Road now is the Grand, standing beyond West Street. It is an immensely attractive building, built in the Italianate style. This was the scene of the infamous IRA bomb in 1984, a modern day gunpowder plot, when the Irish Republican Army planted a bomb in room 629, timed to detonate at 2.45 am, when the Conservative Party was holding its annual conference next door at the Brighton Centre. The plan was to assassinate Prime Minister Margaret Thatcher, wipe out as many ministers of her cabinet as possible and so further the cause of self-rule for Northern Ireland. Mrs Thatcher escaped injury, (only because she worked late) but five people died, thirty-four were injured and the hotel was wrecked by a chimneystack that fell through several floors taking anything and everything with it. One MP slept through the whole event. The repair bill was £11 million and the roofline of the hotel is now mostly of plastic, to minimise damage by debris if anything like a bomb should go off again.

The Grand opened in 1864 and was one of the first hotels anywhere in the country to be fitted with lifts (called 'ascending omnibuses'). Two early rules were that no pipe smoking was allowed and guests could not take their own pianos into the hotel. Many famous people stayed here over the years, such as Louis Napoleon III, King Edward VII, Sir Winston Churchill, President John Kennedy and Ronald Reagan – in his acting days.

The Metropole Hotel in its original form

The Metropole, the huge building beyond the Grand, to the west, is a marvellous piece of assertive architecture by Alfred Waterhouse, the celebrated Victorian designer, responsible for, among other things, the Natural History Museum in South

The Metropole today

Kensington, London. Its red-brick colour was audacious in 1890 (when it was opened), as every other building on the seafront then was cream-coloured. Originally, the hotel had a much livelier roofline than the flat, plain one you see today, with a central spire and pavilions on it, but this was all lost in 1960, when the owners shamefully flattened it for a new restaurant and additional bedrooms. The famous who have stayed here have included actors Sir Ralph Richardson, Richard Burton and Elizabeth Taylor, Sir Winston Churchill and singer Barry Manilow. John

Brighton Centre

Haigh, an infamous British serial killer, stayed at the hotel in the 1940s. He was known as the 'acid bath murderer', as he disposed of his victims by dissolving them in sulphuric acid. A Metropole doorman, retiring in 1987, recalled Haigh as being 'a perfect gentleman!'

Further west, near the West Pier, is the Hilton Brighton West Pier Hotel (what a mouthful!), an awful slab tower, opened in 1967 to replace a really elegant, stylish 1829 building which burnt down in 1964. Charles Dickens, the most famous guest at the original hotel, wrote much of *Dombey and Son* and *Bleak House* there. Dickens was a frequent visitor to Brighton between 1837 and 1868.

The building at the bottom of West Street, looking like a cream-coloured box with a gold crown on top, is the Kingswest entertainment centre – a multi-screen cinema and disco complex – and it's hoped that this dire example of 1960s kitsch will come down very soon. Another architectural blight is the Brighton Centre, the town's main entertainment building and conference facility, which despite excellent amenities inside, is a featureless, blank building, which typifies grey, 1970s architecture at its worst.

Many celebrated entertainers have performed here, including Tom Jones, Michael Crawford, Cliff Richard, Shirley Bassey, Bob Dylan and nearly every contemporary pop group. American crooner, Bing Crosby, gave his last public performance here, in 1979. There is a plaque inside the building relating to this. The centre also stages many top sporting events, including basketball, tennis and snooker. There is an ice-skating show each winter, where a temporary rink is created on the floor of the main hall.

In the other direction (some way to the east), the Thistle Hotel (first called the Ramada) is another unfortunate modern building, opened in 1987.

Near Brighton Pier is the Queen's Hotel. Previously on this site was a bath building, the first, it's said, to offer Turkish baths anywhere in the country. Bath buildings flourished in Brighton in the wake of the sea-water cure, the main benefit being that bathing could take place all-year round, irrespective of the weather or conditions outside. Mahomed's Baths, as they were called, were opened by Sake Dene Mahomed, a real Brighton character, in 1815.

This building originally overlooked the sea; the road to the south – first called Grand Junction Parade – wasn't opened until 1829. Sake Dene Mahomed, from Patna, also performed shampooing, which then meant vigorous massage, performed while the 'patient' wore only a kind of flannel tent, with internal sleeves, whereby the masseur could reach in and get to the part (or parts)

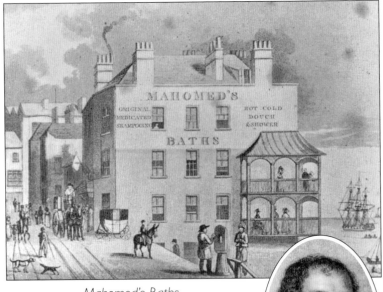

Mahomed's Baths

needing massage. He became 'Shampooing Surgeon' to George IV, at the Royal Pavilion, and his successor, William IV. The entrance hall of his premises was festooned with the crutches, walking sticks, artificial legs and other discarded aids of patients he had 'cured' of their afflictions. There must have been something to his methods as Sake Dene himself died in 1851, aged 102. Hotel premises replaced his baths in 1870.

Sake Dene Mahomed

Very close to the Queen's Hotel is Dr Brighton's, just a pub now, but in the past a characterful hotel dating from the 1790s. It was William Thackeray who dubbed the town 'kind, cheerful, merry Doctor Brighton', and this pub takes its name from that quip.

This guide could be filled ten times over with stories about Brighton's seafront and hotels, but it now moves on to look at some of the streets bounded by East Street, North Street and West Street, starting with what's known as The Lanes area.

This is a series of extremely attractive walkways in the centre of the Old Town area, probably built up from the late 1500s. Again, refer to the map for the exact location. Tiny cottages existed here once, populated by fishermen and their families. Today, refronted or completely rebuilt, they house all manner of antique shops, restaurants, boutiques, pubs and art galleries. This area was once called the Hempshares, where hemp was grown to make rope for the fishermen. In 1964, a circular stone tank, twelve feet across, found in the

Entrance to The Lanes

basement of a shop in the Lanes, was once used for soaking the hemp, to make its fibres separate easily.

Uncovering the hemp soak

Only a few buildings are of any great age in The Lanes, although many Victorian frontages conceal older structures behind and some old fireplaces and parts of walls are much too big or thick for the size of building they are in, so are thought to have incorporated parts of older buildings, even remains of an extensive priory that once stood on the site, but which was burnt down in 1514 during one of the French raids mentioned earlier, and

The haunted arch

which survived, as ruins, until the 1590s.

As you would expect, The Lanes is an extremely haunted area (like the rest of Brighton), the most celebrated phantom being a spectral woman who glides up Meeting House Lane, then melts through a bricked up arch (easily found, by the gate of the Friends Meeting House). The best sighting was in World War II, during the blackout, when a woman on fire-watch duty pursued the apparition some distance up the lane, then watched her disappear into the arch.

Two fishermen saw a ghostly form here in the 1950s. More recently, a strange mist appeared at the arch in the late 1970s, on a suitably spooky autumn day and a motorbike propped against the wall crashed over at the same time. It used to be thought that the spectre was a nun, connected with the old priory building once on the site, but more recent sightings seem to make her a woman with a shawl over her head. She appeared at the Font and Firkin pub, just round a corner or two from the arch, in late 1995.

The shops of The Lanes are unendingly fascinating as a morning or afternoon's saunter will soon prove. Several pubs and restaurants are at hand, where you can take a break and watch everyone else go by. Some of the more specialist shops are amazing; at the time of writing this guide two shops deal in collector's teddy bears, one sells antique weapons, another Art Deco furnishings.

Brighton Square in The Lanes, is a development of the mid-1960s and won awards at the time for how well its new buildings blended with the old. Another good place to sit and watch the dolphin fountain and refresh yourself.

If The Lanes beguile you by day, you should also visit them at night. In *Unknown Brighton*, published in 1926, a rather charming description of The Lanes runs:

To see the Lanes at their best you should visit them at that magic hour when twilight is deepening into night. The shadows that have been lurking there for centuries slide from their corners and throw their dark hoods over the old houses. The queer old places seem to be falling asleep, as well they might after their busy days for

Brighton Square

century following century. They nod, and lean forward their upper storeys as if seeking the support of their neighbours while they drowse. Perhaps in the darkness they are whispering secrets – of the raids by the French, of the adventures of Charles, of the amours of Prince George.

Shops in The Lanes

Fanciful stuff? Well, yes, but visit The Lanes at this time and you just might find yourself thinking there's something in it.

Moving out of The Lanes, this guide now looks at some of the interesting streets nearby (still in the Old Town area). All these streets, except probably Middle Street, came into existence following the rebuilding of the town from 1545 onwards (after the French attack that year), although hardly anything in them is of any great age.

MIDDLE STREET

Naturally enough, this street was once right in the middle of the Old Town, between East Street and West Street, so that's how it got its name. Today it contains several notable buildings. Its most splendid, though it doesn't look it from the outside, is Brighton's Synagogue, on the eastern side, near the seaward end. Built in 1874-75, in a strange, but somehow fitting Byzantine style, this has the finest interior of any synagogue in Europe. It is open to the public at various times and if you can get in, you will be

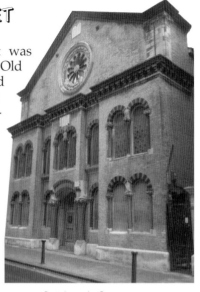

Brighton's Synagogue

Interior of the synagogue

truly amazed by what you find.

Another interesting building, on the western side, further up, almost at the top, is a school building dating from 1971. This is Middle Street School which, although now in modern premises, was founded on the site in 1805, the year of the Battle of Trafalgar. On the same side, below Boyces Street, is a bow-fronted building, a hostel for backpackers. Here, William Friese-Greene made films and devised and patented a large number of cinematic devices, when Hollywood was in its infancy and known only for its orange groves. Actor Michael Redgrave unveiled the plaque on the wall here in 1951. This coincided with the release of a film about Friese-Greene, called *The Magic Box*, in which Redgrave appeared. However, Friese-Greene is something of a shadowy figure now

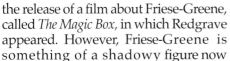

The Friese-Greene house

and film historians find it hard to point to anything really specific he produced that was pivotal in cinema development; he certainly isn't considered the father of modern cinema as it says on the plaque.

The most famous building in Middle Street, opposite the Friese-Greene house, is the Hippodrome. Between 1901 and 1964, this was Brighton's principal variety theatre. Everyone, but everyone, appeared here, from Laurel and Hardy to Laurence Olivier, Houdini to Judy Garland. Again, just think of any great variety act, dance band or solo performer and they're sure to have played the 'Hippo'. The Beatles gave two concerts here in 1964, just before the place closed. Among other pop stars

The Hippodrome in 1905

to appear were the Rolling Stones, Cliff Richard, Dusty Springfield and Adam Faith.

As with many theatres in the 1960s, its closure was due to the impact of television and the gradual dying of twice-nightly variety shows. The Hippodrome became a TV recording studio for a short period (Liza Minnelli was filmed performing there) before being converted in 1967 to the bingo hall it is today.

DUKE STREET

The top, northern end of Middle Street comes out into Duke Street, which is not so interesting as Middle Street, but has a lot of up-

market shops and still the odd tale to tell. About half way up on the northern side is a low cream-coloured restaurant, which stands on the site of Brighton's second theatre, built in 1790 and closed in 1806. Several notable performers appeared here, including the great Sarah Siddons, the Judi Dench of her day.

But the great sensation at this Duke Street theatre, in 1793, was the outrageous fencer, the Chevalier D'Eon, who

The Duke Street Theatre in the eighteenth century, right; the site today, above

gave displays of fancy sword fighting dressed as a woman. 'All the world wondered,' we read, 'whether the fencer was man or woman. Curiosity to see 'the lady' was wrought up to the highest pitch; and never was there such excitement at the theatre since it had been opened.' The 'Chevalier' was, in reality, very male and earned a substantial living touring and teasing in this way.

SHIP STREET

Ship Street runs north-south across the Old Town area and contains several entrances into The Lanes area. There isn't a lot of interest in the street, not today anyway. It takes its name from the Old Ship Hotel on its seafront corner, which to start with was just called 'The Ship'. The hotel changed to the Old Ship because a rival hotel opened on the other side of the street (about the middle of the 1600s) calling itself the New Ship. Neither proprietor wanted patrons getting the two mixed up, so the earlier hotel was prefixed 'Old'.

In 1790 a party of thirty-seven elderly nuns turned up at the New Ship, having been driven by persecution from their convent in Lisle, northern France, during the French Revolution. They arrived by packet steamer, with only £30 between them. The Prince of Wales and Mrs Fitzherbert set up a subscription which raised £100 for the nuns. The landlord of the Old Ship, a Mr Balcombe, was hard-pressed to accommodate them during their stay however, because he could not persuade them to sleep two to a bed. In 1805, this same Balcombe won a lottery prize of £20,000 (an incredible sum of money to win

The New Ship in the 1920s

then) but he had to share his prize with sixteen others. Despite this money, he stayed on at the Old Ship, as host, for several more years.

The New Ship has been rebuilt three times and stands today as a large bar and restaurant on the western side of Ship Street, very near the seafront road. Further up, on the same side of Ship Street, just before the turn into Duke Street, there is a small street of attractive shops, known as Dukes Lane. This appears old and quaint, but is in fact a 1970s assemblage of buildings, arranged like a Victorian Street but with the feel of a film set.

BLACK LION STREET

This is another very ancient thoroughfare, leading down to the sea, but one that has suffered dreadfully from modern redevelopment. There are only two interesting buildings left, both pubs, standing at the northern end, on the western side and close to the start of The Lanes. One is the Cricketers, the frontage of which is 1820s, but inside is far older.

The Cricketers is easily the most atmospheric pub in the city. It's best sampled on a wet, windy night, when all is snug inside; you then half expect fishermen from the past to come bursting in, all wet oilskins and sou'westers, saying there's a ship wrecked down

The Cricketers

on the beach below the cliff and there's pickings to be had! The pub was named by Thomas Jutten, proprietor from 1790 and a cricket fanatic. Before this, it had the curious name of The Last and Fishcart (a 'last' being fisherman's slang for 10,000 fish).

The other pub, next to it, on the southern side of Black Lion Lane, is on the site of an ancient brewery

The Black Lion Brewery a century ago

which existed from Tudor times through to the late 1960s. A large part of the original structure lasted until the 1930s. In its day, it was the oldest brewery building in the world, dating from the rebuilding of the town, following the French attack and sacking of 1545.

The old photograph, of the early 1900s, shows the street frontage of the brewery more or less in its original Tudor condition. A legend persists that this brewery was owned by Deryck Carver, burnt at the stake at Lewes in the reign of Mary Tudor (Henry VIII's eldest daughter, and known as Bloody Mary). The Queen sought to return the country to Catholicism; her father, of course,

Site of the brewery today

was founder of the Church of England. During the persecutions of her reign, Carver, a Protestant, was arrested, imprisoned for seven months, then martyred in 1555. He made a defiant speech, flinging his Bible into the crowd, before being consumed by the flames. However, it's now thought Carver owned the Black Lion Inn, a quite different building, which was on the other side of the street, demolished about 1815. The modern pub, on the site of the brewery, has a plaque on it, detailing Carver's connection with the building, but this was added to the wall in the 1920s, when the old story still persisted.

Black Lion Lane is well worth walking down (it leads to Ship Street, where another narrow walkway, Ship Street Gardens, takes you to Middle Street). Black Lion Lane is probably where a famous race took place (related on page 25). Along this lane are some ancient, tiny houses, which are believed to date from the 1600s, although they have been refronted and altered a fair bit down the years.

MARKET STREET AND BRIGHTON PLACE

The Town Hall

Market Street originally ended at King's Road, but was blocked off by building of the Thistle (Ramada) Hotel in 1987. One way into the street is to turn off East Street (west) at a place called Bartholomews, and pass the Town Hall. This was built between 1830 and 1831, smaller than intended, and it soon proved impractical to hold all the departments needed by those responsible for local government in the town. It did have a large hall, which was used for municipal events; Madame Tussaud hired it, to exhibit her wax figures, in 1832.

The Druid's Head

Edward II allowed Brighton to hold a weekly market and fair in 1313. The last market buildings actually in Market Street were cleared in the 1930s. A century before, a market had wives for sale. One woman was offered for five shillings (25p) plus eight quarts of beer. This practice continued, intermittently, for a number of years, and it's said that author Thomas Hardy, on a visit to Brighton, recorded details of wife-selling in the town and used the information for a scene in his novel, *The Mayor of Casterbridge* (1886).

Brighton Place opens out from Market Street and is where the Druid's Head pub stands along with a number of restaurants and designer shops. Brighton Square, in The Lanes, is just round a corner (left). In fact there are several ways into The Lanes on the western side of Market Street. Brighton Place was called the Knab in ancient times (another Saxon word, meaning 'rising ground'). It was pedestrianised as recently as 1989.

The Druid's Head is the most ancient pub here, dating from the 1820s, although the building itself, faced with knapped flint, is probably much older. It's haunted of course!

CASTLE SQUARE

Follow Market Street as far as you can, beyond Brighton Place, pass the Pump House and keeping right you'll come out at the top of East Street, near Castle Square, very close to the Royal Pavilion entrance here.

The most important building here, from which Castle Square took its name, was the opulent Castle Hotel and Ballroom, opened in the 1750s (enlarged in 1766), in response to the demand among wealthy visitors for afternoon and evening entertainment. It offered card games, balls, dinners, dancing, concerts, masquerades, all good opportunities for gossip and seeing who was with whom. When the waltz was introduced here, in the early 1800s, it was perfectly suited to the lecherous mood of the period; a man could have his hand on a woman's back in public, half embrace her and occasionally brush up against her bosom, not just hold her fingertips and childishly skip about, as in the 'up the sides and down the middle' dances of old.

Top, the Castle Hotel; above, a bank occupies the site today

The Old Ship Hotel offered similar diversions and for a while the two coexisted. Eventually the crowds favoured the Old

Ship, leading to the closure and subsequent demolition of the Castle Hotel in 1823. A terrace of houses was built on the site the following year and was subsequently converted into a large department store. This went in 1930 for road-widening, and the present building, currently a bank, opened in 1932.

OLD STEINE

Castle Square opens out to the east at Old Steine, a large open space of fine gardens, with an ornate fountain in the centre of the lower section and Brighton's war memorial largely occupying the upper. The fountain was unveiled in 1846, to mark Queen Victoria's twenty-seventh birthday. The road through the middle, now full of traffic, was first laid out in 1824.

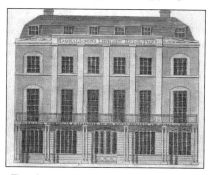

Originally, the Steine was just a large open space used by fishermen as a drying ground for their nets. The word *steine* is of Saxon deri-vation, meaning 'rock' or (depending on your source)

The Steine Library, in the eighteenth century, and below, in 1934

'place of stones'. There used to be, it's said, a ledge of chalk rocks at the southern end of the ground, near the sea, which gave the area its name. The Wellesbourne river ran through the Steine until 1793, when it was enclosed in an underground sewer. With the coming of wealthy, fashionable visitors from the 1750s onwards, seeking the sea-water cure and other diversions, the Steine became an area for 'promenading', which meant walking about, chatting, flirting mildly and people-watching. It was surrounded by iron railings in 1823 and lit by gas the following year. The first proper building to go up was a library, in 1760, which, subsequently rebuilt, existed until the 1930s.

Fine, large houses were constructed from 1780, forming the parades that are still in place on the eastern side today. All this development meant the fishermen had to move off the Steine (and they didn't half protest about it) and dry their nets by draping them over the seafront railings, the start of the gradual decline of fishermen's rights in the town, ending as recently as 1960, when their market on the lower promenade was closed and they were forced off the seafront for good (no fishermen operate from Brighton beach today).

During Regency times many eccentrics and weird people could be found in the Steine area, the most celebrated being 'The Green Man'. This was Henry Cope, a small man who dressed entirely in green, went around in a green carriage, painted the rooms of his home green and who, in an age when no-one had heard the word 'vegetarian', ate only fruit and green vegetables. In 1806, having become even more deranged than usual, he threw himself off the cliff at Brighton, but somehow survived and was taken to London, to be looked after by friends.

A somewhat snide little rhyme was made up about the Green Man:

> A spruce little man in a doublet of green,
> Perambulates daily the streets and the Steyne,
> Green striped is his waistcoat, his small clothes are green,
> And oft round his neck a green 'kerchief is seen.
>
> Green watch string, green seals, and for certain I've heard,
> (Tho' they're powdered) green whiskers and eke a green beard;
> Green garters, green hose, and deny it who can,
> The brains too are green of this little green man!

Several buildings surrounding the Steine have blue, circular plaques on them, meaning that someone famous is connected with the building. On the eastern side of the Steine, roughly in line with the fountain, is number 30, where Gideon Mantell lived from 1833 to 1838. Who was he? He was a doctor, but keen amateur geologist and was first to discover fossil remains of the iguanodon dinosaur – the one with a spiky 'thumb'.

Often called 'the finest house in Brighton', Robert Adam's classical villa, known as Marlborough House, is on the western side of the lower Steine area. The first house on this site was built in 1769 as the residence for Samuel Shergold, proprietor of the Castle Ballroom. He sold it to the fourth Duke of Marlborough in 1771 (which shows the calibre of resident the town was attracting at this time, thirteen years before the Prince of Wales' first visit). He employed some forty servants, and the left-overs from banquets were given away to the poor and

Mrs Fitzherbert's house

needy. When the house was sold again, in 1786, Adam remodelled both the inside and the outside to what can be seen today. In more recent times the house served as Brighton's tourist information centre (currently in Bartholomew Square, by the Town Hall), but now, recently restored, it stands as the most stylish office building anywhere along the south coast.

Mrs Fitzherbert lived in a house on the Steine from 1804 (when it was built) to 1837, and it's still there, although refronted in the 1920s. Built by William Porden, who designed the Dome stables, it's on the western side, at the corner of Steine Lane, serving as a YMCA building. Sadly, it no longer contains the great staircase up which Lord Barrymore rode his horse.

The Royal Pavilion

PAVILION ESTATE

Round the corner from Castle Square, north, past the bus stops, is the Pavilion estate and here you will see the rear of the Royal Pavilion. A walk either back through Castle Square or right round the rear of the building (follow the wall) will bring you to the Pavilion grounds and the main entrance of the palace. Standing viewing the building, you may wonder how best to describe this oriental fantasy when you get back home (if you're visiting that is). All manner of comments have been made on the Pavilion since it was built, ranging from ecstatic praise and snide witticisms to downright abuse. The venomous Anthony Pasquin (whom we met earlier), said of the first, smaller, Marine Pavilion: 'It is a nondescript monster in building, and appears like a madhouse, or a house run mad, as it hath no beginning, middle, nor end'. What he thought of the final version doesn't bear thinking about.

William Hazlitt, writing in 1826 (of the final version), said: 'The

Pavilion at Brighton is like a collection of stone pumpkins and pepperboxes. It seems as if the genius of architecture had at once the dropsy and the megrims'.

The most cutting comment on the Pavilion was by famous wit Sydney Smith, the curate of St Paul's Cathedral in London. When he saw the building, not long after it was completed, he quipped: 'One would think the dome of St Paul's had come to Brighton … and pupped!'

But whatever was said in the past, the Pavilion is now rightly admired by all who see it as the most fantastic palace in Europe. Its interior décor teeters somewhere between the utterly sublime and the unreservedly ridiculous. No one should visit Brighton without going inside. A good place to end this guide.

AND THE REST

There you have it, a nippy guide to one area of what is the most unique seaside resort in the country. It's quite a story. But this little book is probably the most incomplete ever published on any city in Britain because there is so much more to the place. A short list now follows of some other buildings that the visitor may like to take in.

There's no doubt that the city of Brighton and Hove possesses the finest seaside architecture anywhere in the country. To find its massive squares and crescents, you need to go either to Kemp Town, well east of the area covered in this guide, or to the Brighton-Hove border, west of the area.

At Kemp Town stands the massive and almost overwhelming Lewes Crescent, with Sussex Square to the north of it, terracing on either side, and landscaped gardens in the centre. You can reach it by travelling on Volk's Railway, the oldest electric railway in the world, from its terminus east of the Brighton Pier entrance. Get off at the end of the ride and the slopes of the estate are opposite, with the buildings across the top road.

Built in stages, the Kemp Town estate is one of the largest in the country and was originally going to be at least twice the size. The attraction of this kind of estate was that a buyer would have a large, comfortable house to live in, but because of all the others in terracing either side of it, the house was made to look like the part of a classical palace. Kemp Town was created in the early 1820s by Thomas Read Kemp, a wealthy landowner and speculator, who wanted to built a large, new, self-sufficient district of Brighton. He employed architects Amon Wilds and Charles

Augustus Busby to work out the general plan and to design the house frontages. The frontages were completed by 1828, except for those along its seafront 'wings' (Chichester Terrace), which were added some twenty-five years later. Various developers then completed the insides of the houses, and as they employed different builders, most ended up with different interior layouts. The best-known of these developers was Thomas Cubitt, who built thirty-seven of the 106 houses. Many weren't finished for twenty or thirty years though, and remained held up by scaffolding.

Thomas Read Kemp
as a young man

Lewes Crescent

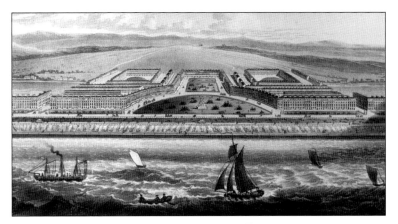

Original design for the Kemp Town estate

The truly spectacular Brunswick Terrace and Square (named after Caroline of Brunswick, the Prince of Wales' unfortunate wife), isn't far from the West Pier, but actually stands in Hove. The eastern part of Brunswick Terrace, built in sections, dates from 1825-28. The square went up at the same time, but the western terrace is later, 1827-30. The whole unit was going to be called

Brunswick Terrace

Embassy Court

Brunswick Town (like Kemp Town) and again, the intention was to build a complete, self-supporting district. The architects were once more Busby and Wilds. Adjoining the eastern terrace is Embassy Court, a block of flats tacked on the eastern extremity during the 1930s. This is an important building, one of the first of 'the modern movement', designed in Art Deco style with its bulk resembling an ocean liner. However, it's completely out of place where it stands and there have been many calls in recent years for it to be demolished, despite recent renovation.

Is there a museum of Brighton, or something similar, where visitors can see more of the city's amazing history? Sadly, there isn't. A Brighton museum was planned in the 1980s, to be housed in a redundant church in Ship Street, appropriately in the Old Town area, but the plan fell through and nothing came of it. The city's museum, in Church Street, not far from the northern end of the Pavilion, has recently been revamped, and does have a few sections to do with Brighton's history on show.

Brighton possesses a quite extraordinary range of churches, the best of them dating from the nineteenth century, financed, as already said, by father and son Wagner. The most dazzling and 'must-see' is St Bartholomew's in Ann Street, just off London Road, completed in 1874. The architectural trick here was creating an interior of stunning beauty, through the severest of structural arrangements. It is a 'one-off' and worth the half-hour walk, or short ride northwards, to see it. It's taller than

Interior of St Bartholomew's

Westminster Abbey in London and nearly always open. You'll probably pass St Peter's Church *en route* (designed by a Charles Barry, architect of the Houses of Parliament) which is also pretty good, but don't get the two churches muddled – they're very close neighbours.

Brighton's first church, on the hill outside the Old Town area (seen on the Tudor drawing, page 5), can be reached by passing

Church of St Bartholomew

Church of St Nicholas

the Clock Tower and travelling up Dyke Road. It's almost immediately on the right. St Nicholas was built above and beyond the Old Town to prevent coastal erosion from claiming it. Although it dates from the fourteenth century, it was so over-restored by zealous Victorians (in 1853) that only the pillars and arches of the nave, the chancel arch and the tower are genuinely ancient. You probably won't be able to get into the church, which is a pity as there are several interesting monuments inside, including one to the Duke of Wellington, who attended the church as a child. There's also a small tablet recording grumpy Dr Johnson's association with the building, and in the floor is the tomb of Ralph Thrale, son of Henry and Hester Thrale, the couple mentioned in the West Street section, who died in 1775.

Outside, in the churchyard you'll find (after a bit of a search) the graves of several Brighton characters mentioned in this guide, including those of Martha Gunn, Amon Wilds, Nicholas Tettersell and Sake Dene Mahomed. Sake Dene's headstone is round the back where it can be glimpsed, but not approached, due to a locked gate. Near the top entrance to the churchyard is the grave of Anna Maria Crouch, one of the Prince of Wales' mistresses. Smoaker Miles is also buried somewhere in the churchyard, but the site of his grave has somehow been lost.

Preston Manor

Moving much further out of central Brighton, if you want to visit a nice haunted house, Preston Manor, on the northern outskirts of the city (just off the main road to London) can boast of many apparitions over the years (some in broad daylight and some very recently). The council advertises it as an Edwardian country mansion (although it is older). Its most famous owners were the Stanford family, from 1794 until 1932. There was a séance here in 1896, following the appearance of a female ghost that spoke to a colonel in the entrance hall. She said she was an ex-communicated nun, who had been buried outside holy ground with no religious ceremony. A few months later, the plumbing system packed up at the house and in digging around to see why, yes, you've guessed it, the bones of a woman were found. Once these had been buried in the nearby churchyard, sightings of the ghost stopped … although plenty of other spectres were, and still are, seen.

Chris Horlock was born, brought up and educated in Brighton, but now lives in Shoreham, a town on the coast a few miles to the west. He works as a full-time teacher in a Worthing school where he is head of history and geography. He has compiled five photographic books on Brighton, gives frequent talks on the city's history, has appeared on television several times and owns a vast archive of Brighton photographs, prints and ephemera.